TULSA CITY-COUNTY LIBRARY

baje
12
11

D1569387

BALLS, BIRDIES & PUCKS

MARY ELIZABETH SALZMANN

Consulting Editor, Diane Craig, M.A./Reading Specialist

A Division of ABDO

ABDO
Publishing Company

visit us at www.abdopublishing.com

Published by ABDO Publishing Company, a division of ABDO, P.O. Box 398166, Minneapolis, Minnesota 55439. Copyright © 2012 by Abdo Consulting Group, Inc. International copyrights reserved in all countries. No part of this book may be reproduced in any form without written permission from the publisher. SandCastle™ is a trademark and logo of ABDO Publishing Company.

Printed in the United States of America, North Mankato, Minnesota
062011
092011

 PRINTED ON RECYCLED PAPER

Editor: Katherine Hengel
Content Developer: Nancy Tuminelly
Design and Production: Anders Hanson
Image research: Stacy Nesbitt
Photo Credits: Shutterstock

Library of Congress Cataloging-in-Publication Data
Salzmann, Mary Elizabeth, 1968-
  Balls, birdies & pucks / Mary Elizabeth Salzmann.
    p. cm. -- (Sports gear)
  ISBN 978-1-61714-822-4
  1. Balls (Sporting goods)--Juvenile literature. 2. Sporting goods--Juvenile literature. I. Title.
GV749.B34S35 2012
688.7′6--dc22
                    2010053046

SANDCASTLE™ LEVEL: TRANSITIONAL

SandCastle™ books are created by a team of professional educators, reading specialists, and content developers around five essential components—phonemic awareness, phonics, vocabulary, text comprehension, and fluency—to assist young readers as they develop reading skills and strategies and increase their general knowledge. All books are written, reviewed, and leveled for guided reading, early reading intervention, and Accelerated Reader® programs for use in shared, guided, and independent reading and writing activities to support a balanced approach to literacy instruction. The SandCastle™ series has four levels that correspond to early literacy development. The levels are provided to help teachers and parents select appropriate books for young readers.

Emerging Readers	Beginning Readers	Transitional Readers	Fluent Readers
(no flags)	*(1 flag)*	*(2 flags)*	*(3 flags)*

CONTENTS

What Are...

BALLS, BIRDIES & PUCKS ?

Balls, birdies, and pucks are sports gear.

They can be used in different ways. They can be thrown, caught, kicked, or hit.

BASEBALL & SOFTBALL

Baseballs and softballs are a lot alike. Players throw and catch them. They also hit them with bats.

SOFTBALL

BASEBALL

Baseballs are smaller than softballs.

A baseball has
108 red **stitches**.

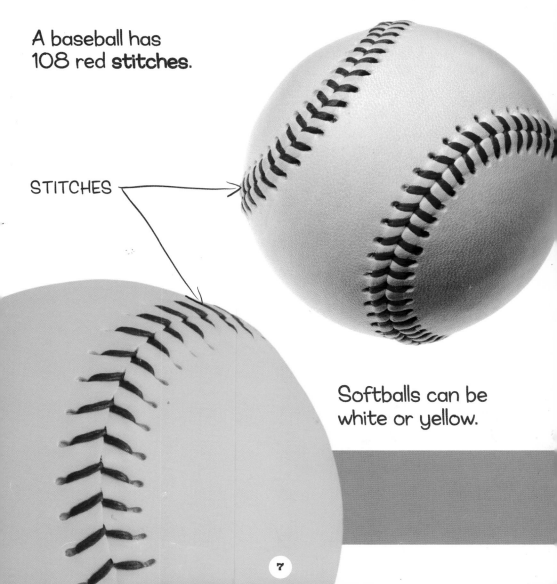

STITCHES

Softballs can be
white or yellow.

BASKETBALL

Basketball players **bounce** the ball on the ground. They also throw and shoot the ball.

The lines on a basketball are called ribs.

RIBS

A men's basketball is bigger than
a women's basketball.

SOCCER BALL

Soccer players kick the ball. They also hit it with their heads, chests, and knees.

A soccer ball has panels.

PANELS

Most soccer balls are black and white.

Soccer balls come in different sizes. Adults use bigger balls. Kids use smaller ones.

FOOTBALL

In football, the players carry the ball.
They also throw, catch, and kick it.

LACES

STITCHES

A football has laces. The laces have eight **stitches**.

A football is not round. It is oval with pointed ends.

TENNIS BALL

Tennis players hit tennis balls with **rackets**.

Tennis balls are made of rubber. They are covered with **felt**.

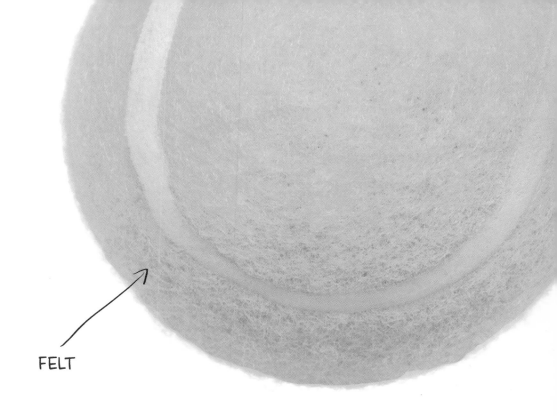

FELT

Most tennis balls are bright yellow.

GOLF BALL

A golf ball is one of the smallest balls used in sports.

Golf balls are covered with small, round dots called dimples.

A golf ball has between 300 and 500 dimples.

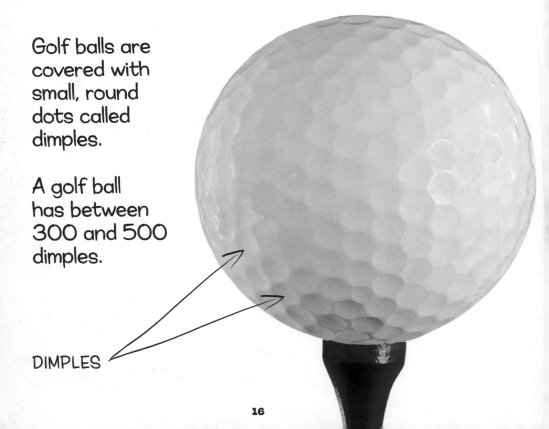

DIMPLES

Golfers hit golf balls with clubs.

BADMINTON BIRDIE

Badminton players hit birdies with **rackets**.

A badminton birdie has a **cork** and rubber base.

There are feathers **attached** to the base.

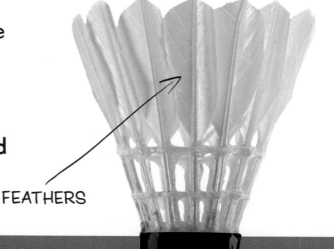

FEATHERS

BASE ⟶

CONE →

Badminton birdies are shaped like cones.

HOCKEY PUCK

Ice hockey players hit pucks
with hockey sticks.

Hockey pucks are made of rubber.

Most hockey pucks are black.

FUN FACTS

- About 60 to 70 baseballs are used during a Major League game.

- Badminton birdies are also called shuttlecocks.

- Hockey pucks are **frozen** before they are used in a game.

QUICK QUIZ

1. A men's basketball is bigger than a women's basketball. True or False?

2. All soccer balls are the same size. True or False?

3. Footballs are round. True or False?

4. The dents on a golf ball are called dimples. True or False?

GLOSSARY

attach – to join things together.

bounce – to throw something down so it hits the floor and springs back up.

cork – a material made out of tree bark.

felt – a soft, thick fabric.

frozen – extremely cold.

racket – a paddle-like tool used in sports to hit things.

stitch – a loop of yarn or thread.